MaPOP
Goes to the Purple Palace

BY

TENAE SHUSH

mapopmovement.life

Praise God from whom all blessings flow.

A Special Thank You To

Noble and Kristie who encouraged me.

TABLE OF CONTENTS

CHAPTER 1
THE SPECIAL DELIVERY

MaPOP is standing in her home, looking out the window. She is feeling giddy and swept away in her thoughts. MaPOP reflects on the unbelievable morning she had just experienced. For the fourth time today, she re-lived every perfect moment of her perfect puppet morning.

It had been unlike any morning before, almost magical.

It all started when MaPOP heard an unexpected knocking at her door. The knock was followed by a man's voice stating, "Special delivery for MaPOP." The voice was not familiar. Before the person on the outside of her door spoke again, MaPOP positioned herself in front of the peephole.

MaPOP asked, "How can I help you?" The man was peculiar, wearing a purple hat with a plume. He had a remarkable and kind smile, it stretched across the whole width of his face.

The man spoke again through the door. "I am here at the request of the Prince and Princess of the Purple Palace."

The words made MaPOP's heart skip. The Purple Palace! What could this possibly mean for her?

MaPOP unlocked the door with pure interest. She stepped back from the threshold after opening it. While curious, MaPOP was plenty glad the man with the purple hat did not try to enter her home. But when she got a good look at him, she was positively convinced this was indeed a man on staff at the Purple Palace.

Not only did he have on a purple hat, but he also wore a purple pleather cape. There was something distinguished and honest about him.

It was as if he carried the very air of the Purple Palace itself, regal, trustworthy, and touched with a hint of mystery.

As he handed MaPOP the special delivery package, MaPOP's puppet mouth opened as wide as it could. She had never seen anything like it before in her puppet life. The package was shaped like the letter "P." It was painted with several fabulous shades of purple.

MaPOP said, "Thank you" to the delivery man. She accepted the delivery, pushed the door closed, and relocked it. It was heavy, but she managed to carry it to the table. MaPOP sighed as she congratulated herself for placing the package safely on the table.

Her heart raced, what could possibly be inside such a peculiar package?

When MaPOP removed the big "P"-shaped lid from the box, she knew it was going to be a great day. Inside the "P"-shaped box were seven smaller packages. She was giddy, yes, very giddy.

She was seated at the short end of her rectangular-shaped table. The bottom part of the special delivery box was closest to her. She reached inside the bigger box and chose the small package closest to her to open first. This box, too, was a fabulous swirl of several hues of purple.

She lifted the lid and immediately smelled the fragrance of roses. There, inside the box, was a small purple potted plant filled with pansies, primroses, petunias, and philodendron. The pot was nestled in a thick bed of fragrant purple rose petals.

The sight took her breath away, it was like opening a garden wrapped in mystery.

MaPOP thought the plant was perfect, even stunning. She promised herself she would take good care of it to keep it alive. She took the plant out of the box gently. She was not sure what to do with the rose petals. They smelled like grape sweet tarts.

MaPOP giggled softly. Who would send such a thoughtful, whimsical gift? And what surprises lay hidden in the other six packages?

She reached for the second box inside the package. The second box was made of wood. It was polished and shiny, and the rings of the wood looked like zigzags. She lifted the lid of the wooden box and stared for a second. Inside the box was a purple musical instrument. She was not sure, but it looked like a piccolo.

When MaPOP picked up the instrument, she placed it between her lips. When she blew air into it, iridescent bubbles came out along with a mellow sound. It was jazzy, almost hypnotic. She laughed, then blew more air into the piccolo until the room was almost filled with bubbles. She moved her fingers as if she knew exactly how to play.

MaPOP continued to stare at the holographic bubbles as they floated above her head. "WOW! Oh my!" exclaimed MaPOP.

The magic of the piccolo lingered in the air, each bubble glowing like a dream she could almost catch.

The third box was the largest of all the boxes. It was half red-violet and half blue-violet. MaPOP was amazed at how well all of the boxes fit inside the "P"-shaped package. She could not imagine what was inside this one.

She lifted the lid. Inside were two poodle puppies. They were the most precious pink and purple plaid poodle puppies anyone had ever laid eyes on. MaPOP scooped them both up into her puppet arms. Each puppy wore a pastel collar around its neck that sparkled.

Her heart melted instantly, the piccolo bubbles still floated around, and now two plaid puppies wriggled in her arms. Could the day get any more unbelievable?

They were playful puppies. After licking her face, they wiggled out of MaPOP's arms and onto the table. They pounced on each other and pranced around all the opened presents, stopping to sniff and lick everything they saw. What a sight!!!

The room was now alive, bubbles still floated above, purple petals scattered across the table, and two plaid poodles turned everything into their playground.

The puppies wore diapers and came with royal puppy food. She had never even imagined plaid poodles. Even as poodles, they were already almost as big as her. As she watched her new friends exploring their new environment, she noticed names on their collars. The collar on the boy poodle read *Phineas.* His sister was named *Presence.* MaPOP guessed they were three to four months old.

Phineas barked a little bark, while Presence tilted her head with curious charm, these were not ordinary puppies. They were royal gifts, full of mystery.

MaPOP's head was beginning to spin because of the extravagant presents she received from the Prince and Princess. She opened the fourth present while keeping a watchful eye on the poodles. This present was wrapped as beautifully as all the others. It was smaller than the rest, a true mini-present.

Inside was a purple pouch. The drawstring closure at the top of the pouch opened easily. MaPOP placed her puppet hand inside cautiously. Inside was another purple pouch. This pouch looked worn, as if it were very old.

MaPOP picked up the pouch and looked inside. She did not know what to make of the contents. Inside the purple pouch were two types of strange objects. They were both shiny and holographic, and they were hard like metals. One had the shape of a smashed pebble, round and flat, a little smaller than an olive. The other shiny object was larger. It had the shape of a small box with no lid, a cube. MaPOP estimated there were about fifteen of each.

The drawstring closure at the top of the pouch opened and closed easily. MaPOP knew at that exact moment she was the happiest puppet in all of Plumville. Plumville is the town MaPOP lives in; it is part of the lands governed by the Prince and Princess of the Purple Palace.

Even though she did not know what all these items were for, she was fairly certain no other puppet in Plumville had a morning like hers. She put the pouch back in the fourth box and replaced the lid.

MaPOP thought out loud, "What else???"

Her voice carried both wonder and disbelief, the morning had already been beyond imagination, yet there were still more gifts waiting.

Before opening the fifth box, MaPOP stopped to reflect on all the presents she had already received. After seeing the potted plant, the piccolo, the plaid puppies, and the pouch of shiny objects, MaPOP laughed to herself, wondering what else she would see. She lifted the lid on the fifth box.

When she opened the fifth box, she pushed her chair back from the table. She was surprised, happy, and perplexed by what she saw inside. Inside the box was a set of purple pearls. These precious gemstones were strung into a beautiful necklace. MaPOP put it around her puppet neck immediately.

After placing the necklace of purple pearls around her neck, she studied the packaging she had pulled them from. It was literally the prettiest box she had ever seen in her puppet life. She reached up to touch the pearls. They were smooth.

Her reflection stared back at her in the shine of the pearls, MaPOP, a puppet draped in treasures from the Purple Palace. For a moment, she felt both royal and small, caught between wonder and disbelief.

The sixth box was also a square. It too was very small. She placed her hand inside the box and looked away for just a moment to check on the puppies. Inside the box she felt a small, hard object. It felt cold, so she thought it was metal.

When she looked in her hand, she saw a small golden heart. On one side of the heart was a beautifully engraved purple "P." She turned the heart over. Inscribed on the other side of the heart it read:

"Weapon of Prayer, for help in need, hold tightly and believe help is on the way."

MaPOP was not sure what to do with this gift. It appeared to be made of fine gold. It was shiny, and it also looked very old.

She held it delicately in her puppet palm, the words echoing in her mind. Unlike the other gifts, this one seemed to carry weight, not of gold, but of meaning.

MaPOP was exhausted after opening the boxes containing the potted plant, piccolo, puppies, pouch, pearls, and now the weapon of prayer. MaPOP wondered why she would ever need a weapon. There was one final surprise waiting to be opened. It was the largest of all the boxes. MaPOP wondered why she had not opened that present first.

When she removed the lid, she screamed out loud, startling the puppies. She put her hands on her face and started repeating again and again, "I don't believe it." Inside the box, the first thing she saw was a very fancy piece of purple paper.

This fancy paper, with fancy writing, was an invitation to the Purple Palace for dinner. MaPOP went puppet wild. She ran around, then twirled as she jumped up and down. MaPOP was elated.

Her dream was no longer just hers, it was real, written in elegant script, sealed with royal intent.

MaPOP stared at the invitation. It read:

"MaPOP, please come for dinner promptly at seven o'clock."

It was signed by the Prince and the Princess. MaPOP did not move after reading the invitation. She just stared straight ahead. When her lips began to move, she stated as if in a dream, "MaPOP has been invited to the Purple Palace."

She lifted the beautiful invitation to admire it. It was then MaPOP noticed there were even more items in the box containing the invitation. Underneath the invitation she saw four more items: a compass, a map, a pocket watch, and a purple envelope.

The gifts no longer felt like simple surprises, they felt like instructions, preparations for a journey beyond anything she had ever known.

The pocket watch had a big letter "P" on its face. Alternating semi-precious stones created a halo around the face of the compass. Attached to the face of the pocket watch was a long gold chain.

The map was unusual. When MaPOP held it in her hand and looked down, she saw a letter "P" with several swirls inside the round part of the "P." However, when she viewed the map from the side, the swirls inside the round part of the letter "P" elevated, suggesting a big hill or a small mountain. MaPOP thought the elevation was just more decoration.

But deep inside, she wondered, was it decoration, or was it a clue?

Finally, she looked at the only item that had not been opened in the seventh box. The outside of the purple envelope read "Special Instructions." When she turned it over, she saw a purple wax seal.

MaPOP broke the seal, opened the envelope, and pulled out the piece of paper inside. She looked at the paper and understood these were special instructions for traveling to the Purple Palace. There were five of them:

1. The compass always points to the Purple Palace.
2. Never trust anything Peril says.
3. When in doubt or trouble, use Weapon of Prayer.
4. Always stay on the Pebbled Path.
5. Please arrive at the Palace promptly at 7:00 p.m.

MaPOP read the list again, her puppet eyes wide. Each line felt like both a promise and a warning. The adventure had not only begun, it was already mapped out.

MaPOP returned the travel instructions back to the fancy envelope. As she looked at all the precious gifts from the Palace spread across the table, she said with conviction and passion, "I am going to the Purple Palace for dinner."

MaPOP began to make a checklist of what she needed to do to prepare for her journey. She instructed herself: dinner, sleep, breakfast, pack my backpack and snacks, see if the neighbor could keep an eye on the puppies and plant, then leave for the Palace at sunrise.

MaPOP left all the presents on the table. She skipped through her apartment onto her patio and dropped into a chair. The two plaid poodles followed her. She looked far to the horizon. Far, far away she could see the outline of the Purple Palace. She scooped up the puppies, enjoying the last few rays of sunlight. She put food in a dish and created a safe temporary area where they could play and rest.

MaPOP was too excited to eat dinner. She hoped to get a goodnight sleep. As she settled in bed, she thought of the things she would need to do. She revisited her list. She recalled she planned to leave the plant and puppies with her very nice neighbor. Just as she drifted off to sleep, MaPOP thought it had been both a peculiar and a perfect day. She smiled a pleasant smile, turned on her puppet side, and drifted off to sleep. She was exhausted.

As she drifted into dreamland, she mumbled, "Tomorrow MaPOP is going to the Purple Palace by invitation of the Prince and Princess." Finally, MaPOP closed her eyes to sleep.

Her dreams were filled with swirls of purple, floating bubbles, and laughter. In the distance, the outline of the Purple Palace shimmered brighter and brighter, as though it were calling her name. When the morning light began to peek through her window, MaPOP stirred. A brand-new day had arrived, and with it, her long-awaited journey.

CHAPTER 2
THE ADVENTURE BEGINS

MaPOP was up before sunrise. She just could not sleep. She was ready to travel all by herself to the Palace for dinner. She decided on a plate of pancakes with butter pecan syrup. It was hard to stay focused and eat.

Her excitement bubbled over with every bite, this was not just breakfast, it was the beginning of an adventure.

Next, she put her pearls back on, placed the prayer heart in her pocket, compass, map, pocket watch, and special instructions inside her backpack. As planned, she asked her very nice neighbor Patrice to take care of the potted plant and the puppies until she returned in a day or two. As a thank you, MaPOP shared her pancakes and some of the fragrant purple rose petals.

Patrice laughed for several minutes when she saw the puppies. It seemed to MaPOP they had grown overnight. She went back to her apartment and put on her backpack. She took a deep breath and opened her front door. As she stepped outside the building, she saw the sunlight just piercing the horizon.

The morning air felt fresh and full of promise, as if even the world itself knew this was an important day.

MaPOP knew where the Pebble Path was, but she had never traveled on it. The path was two pastures away. It was quiet except for the sound of happy birds chirping. Their morning chatter announced the new day. The sky surrounding the rising sun was the lightest shade of periwinkle blue. It was certainly going to be a perfect day.

MaPOP clutched her backpack straps and smiled. The Pebbled Path was waiting.

MaPOP crossed the first pasture, waving hello to the farmer as she made her way through the chest-high stalks of corn. The air was warm and filled with the sounds of morning on a farm. A moo-moo here and a quack-quack there. All the barnyard sounds one might expect danced on the morning air. Her thoughts returned to the Pebbled Path.

While she was familiar with the Pebbled Path's approximate location, she realized she had never placed a puppet toe on it. MaPOP was exhilarated as she imagined saying hello to the Prince and Princess. She pretended to bow and curtsy. She did not realize it, but her anticipation led her to increase her pace.

Her steps grew lighter, her heart quicker, every thought of the Purple Palace made her feet dance faster.

As she increased her pace, she began to do her version of pirouettes. She danced, twirling until she was tired. She was now halfway through the second pasture.

MaPOP decided this would be a great place and time to familiarize herself with the travel aids in her backpack. She took off her backpack and perched it on a nearby tree stump.

First, she looked at the pocket watch. She paused for a moment, admiring just how beautiful it was. She observed the two hands on its face were both encrusted with tiny jewels. MaPOP decided to fasten the chain of the pocket watch to her belt loop. Before placing the pocket watch back in her pocket, she noticed the time was 6:45 a.m.

Only a little over eleven hours until dinner at the Palace, her journey had to move forward quickly.

Returning her focus to the contents of the backpack, she pulled out the compass. It too was absolutely fabulous. She thought for a moment, *"I wonder how much all of these presents cost?"*

This compass only pointed in the direction of the Palace. MaPOP tested it. She held it in her hand and turned around in a circle. She kept her eyes on the needle. It moved as she moved, the needle of the compass always pointed toward the Palace.

MaPOP thought to herself, *"It is time to get going."* She knew she was very close to the Pebbled Path. Before she moved, she pulled out the map. She wanted to study it in more detail. After making a mental note of the first town she would see, with renewed determination she said out loud, "I am going to the Purple Palace for dinner."

Before she knew it, she had made it to the Pebbled Path. She paused for a second, then placed her puppet foot on the Pebbled Path.

The moment her foot touched the path, it felt like a promise had been sealed, her journey had officially begun.

As MaPOP advanced toward her destination, a pair of menacing eyes watched her from his window on the Pebbled Path. It was Peril. Peril was watching MaPOP head to the Palace. He had seen her practicing her pirouettes. He kept watching as she advanced up the Pebbled Path.

Peril studied her dancing and prancing. He thought to himself, *"She is so happy, it makes me sick."* He was jealous, and he had a puny heart.

Peril had been to the Purple Palace before, but he made some very poor choices and knew he would never be invited again. While he was at the Palace, by invitation of his cousin Pewter, he stole something very valuable. Then he lied and said he did not. The Prince and Princess made a decree that he was never to be admitted to the royal palace again.

His banishment burned inside him like a wound that never healed.

Peril knew the man who made the special delivery. This is how he found out that MaPOP was invited to the Palace to have dinner with the Prince and Princess. Even though he had stolen from them, he was jealous of MaPOP because he was not invited.

And so, as MaPOP's joyful steps carried her forward, Peril's dark thoughts began to stir, shadowing the path ahead.

Peril was so jealous. He had heard all about the extravagant special delivery invitations for dinner. MaPOP's presence, and every step she took on the Pebbled Path toward the Palace, reminded him that he was not gifted: a plant nestled in purple petals, or a magic piccolo, or two plaid poodle puppies, or a fancy pouch, or a necklace made of pearls. But most importantly, he did not receive an invitation from the Prince and Princess. Peril felt rejected.

Looking back out his window, Peril fixed his sinister gaze on MaPOP. He could see her prancing and dancing on the Pebbled Path as though she did not have a care. It was at that very moment that the pretentious Peril began to plan how he would lead MaPOP astray. Peril decided he would meet her on the Pebbled Path and pretend to be her friend.

Peril thought in his puny heart, *"While walking I will get her to trust me. Then I'll point her in the wrong direction."*

Peril thought if he could not go himself, because he was not invited, then he would have fun preventing MaPOP from arriving on time. Peril moved away from his window and did a crazy, menacing celebratory dance. He knew he would have to get moving because MaPOP was traveling swiftly.

Meanwhile, MaPOP was approaching her first landmark, Platesville. She saw a huge sign pointing the way. MaPOP knew she was headed in the right direction. She saluted herself, yelling, *"Next stop, Platesville!"* MaPOP was so proud of herself for making it all the way to Platesville. Platesville was a village on the Pebbled Path leading MaPOP to the Palace.

Her heart quickened with pride. The Palace no longer felt like a distant dream, it was a journey unfolding step by step. Ahead lay Platesville, a place she had only heard whispers of, but never seen. What wonders would await her there?

CHAPTER 3

THE TOWN OF PLATESVILLE

MaPOP thought to herself, *What a peculiar place.* MaPOP never imagined a town occupied by plates. They all lived in cupboards and cabinets. Actually, all the cupboards, cabinets, carts, credenzas, and bookcases MaPOP saw were painted in the prettiest shades of purple anyone had ever seen. She took in the sight with a pleasing smile. She made a panoramic scan of the place in front of her.

MaPOP took a deep breath and exclaimed, "Wow." To the left, she saw dense wooded lands. Large birds circled the periwinkle blue sky. The air was crisp and clean.

In the center of the panoramic view, MaPOP saw the community of Platesville. From her distance, she could only make out a collection of structures. Looking further to the right of the town center of Platesville, MaPOP noticed a clearing marked off by what appeared to be stringed lights.

The mix of color, light, and sky filled her puppet heart with wonder, this was no ordinary village.

MaPOP hurried her pace.

MaPOP's arrival to Platesville created quite a stir. The closer she moved to what she guessed was the center of Platesville, the more cabinet doors and cupboard drawers of the china cabinets flew wide open. Plates of all types were rolling out of the phenomenal painted cabinets. They were practically flying through the air.

There were plates of all types: fine china plates, paper plates, baby plates, everyday plates, round plates, oval plates, square plates, octagon plates, and triangle plates. There were more plates with stars, plates with cars, plates with confetti, and plates with Santa Claus. There were green plates, gold plates, gingerbread plates, bunny plates, bird plates, banana plates, and brass plates. They just kept coming out of the cabinets.

Finally, the air cleared. MaPOP was a bit surprised, none of the glass or china plates were broken or chipped.

Next, MaPOP saw the strangest sight: the plates were all lined up as though they were preparing to go into battle. But MaPOP had never been so wrong about what her puppet eyes told her was going on.

Just then, a large gold-rimmed plate rolled up by her side. It had a friendly face that shouted with a wide grin, "Welcome, welcome! We are *platety* glad that you are here."

The plates collectively chuckled at the plate humor. The plate speaking to MaPOP giggled too.

MaPOP couldn't help but laugh along, this peculiar town of Platesville was already full of surprises.

Then MaPOP heard a whistle blow, and all the plates stood still, because they knew it was time to do the Platesville drill. These were not just ordinary plates. Collectively, they made up the very famous Prazin' Plates.

The plates were perfectly synchronized, turning first to the left and then to the right. All together, they started to spin. MaPOP thought it was a delight, so she jumped right in.

The music of their movement filled the air, so lively, so joyful, it was impossible to resist.

After they danced, they lifted their hands, opened their mouths, and said, "How glad I am!"

MaPOP took a deep breath and thought to herself, *How beautiful, how perfect, how lovely, how grand.*

MaPOP understood just what they meant, so she let them know about her consent. Without delay, MaPOP became very busy, lifting her arms and clapping her puppet hands. She danced and sang until she was tired, but the plates kept singing for more than an hour.

MaPOP exclaimed as loud as she could, "Can it be true? Tell me, what do I see?"

She thought, *How am I so special?* MaPOP's unbelief was diminished as the plates sang on and danced.

The thought of who these plates were, so unique, so full of joy, made MaPOP start dancing again. She wanted to shout!

MaPOP smiled deep down inside. She exclaimed, "I am with the Prazin' Plates, live!" As the piano played, the air seemed to pulsate. The sopranos and altos were hitting high notes. The tenors and basses rounded out the smooth, full-bodied sound.

Before MaPOP knew it, she had jumped in the middle again. MaPOP pranced and danced with the band. This went on for another hour, but MaPOP had to go. She had to arrive at the Purple Palace by 7:00 p.m. The invitation indicated the arrival time was promptly at 7:00 p.m. MaPOP understood that meant, *please do not be late.*

Her heart tugged between joy and duty, one more song with the Plates, or the journey ahead?

She told them goodbye and moved away from the crowd. Each plate waved goodbye and started to cry. Physically exhausted, MaPOP waved goodbye. She had so much fun, there was a tear in her eye.

The plates did not want her to leave so soon. MaPOP said, "Don't worry, you'll see me real soon."

Before MaPOP left, they placed in her hand two fresh, juicy peaches, not from a can. She placed the fruit in her backpack and checked the time on the pocket watch. Reading 10:45 a.m., she knew it was definitely time to scram.

With peaches in her pack and music still echoing in her ears, MaPOP pressed on.

MaPOP wasted no time returning to the Pebbled Path. She moved forward with a joyful stride. She had no idea Peril was standing back, watching her glide. Peril was being sneaky and planning his lie.

His jealousy of MaPOP grew to a giant size. His envy and pride held him so tightly, he started turning green.

As MaPOP skipped ahead toward her destiny, Peril's envy darkened like a storm cloud behind her.

MaPOP pressed on in pilgrimage to dine with the Prince and Princess. She knew that at the Palace she would have a great time. MaPOP felt good deep down inside. She thought about the purple invitation, presented to her with such style.

Feeling grand as she walked away, MaPOP slipped her hands into both pockets. She felt both the compass and the pocket watch. These were just two of her gifts from the Palace, enclosed with the invitation. She knew to take them with her as she traveled the Pebbled Path. She thought they could help her not get lost.

Moving along, MaPOP followed the Pebbled Path as it curved around a bend. It was then that MaPOP slowed her pace. She saw the silhouette of a strange creature.

When she saw Peril, MaPOP was not afraid. All the joy from Platesville made her brave. MaPOP continued her trot on the path, moving herself closer to the creature.

As she moved closer, she began to study it. Honestly, she did not know whether to be happy or sad. She was not even sure if it was a Mom or a Dad. The creature held eye contact with MaPOP.

MaPOP cautiously crossed over to the side of the Pebbled Path farthest away from the creature. Finally, MaPOP was directly in front of it. It continued to stare at her. MaPOP continued to stare back. They stared at each other.

The air grew still, like time itself was watching.

MaPOP thought the creature was somehow familiar.

But where had she seen those eyes before?

Peril lied to MaPOP right after he said hello. He introduced himself as Pareal (Pa-real). MaPOP introduced herself as MaPOP. They exchanged customary pleasantries. They talked about the beautiful day and the fabulous weather. They both seemed to enjoy the pleasant sound of the chirping birds.

MaPOP did not realize at the time that Pareal, the creature, was really Peril.

MaPOP asked Pareal directly, "Are you headed to the Purple Palace?"

"Oh yes," lied Peril. Next, he said, "In fact, I will be leaving shortly. I just have to grab a few items and I will be on my way."

MaPOP thought for a moment and said, "Are you going by way of the Pebbled Path?"

Peril smiled a sneaky smile. Then he replied, "I will be taking the Pebbled Path most of the way." Then he volunteered more information: "The Pebbled Path has been damaged."

He asked if MaPOP knew it was damaged. Before she could answer him, he blurted out, "I will be going around the damaged part." Then, with the most disingenuous grin, he told MaPOP he was "very glad to meet her."

He stated he needed to pack a few things before he left for the Palace. MaPOP looked away for a second or two. When she attempted to return her gaze to the creature, it was gone. POOF! It had just vanished from view.

MaPOP looked this way and that way, up and down. She even spun around. There was no sign of Peril, who was calling himself Pareal.

The silence felt heavier now, as if the path itself had swallowed him whole.

MaPOP concluded the creature Pareal was very strange and started moving again along the Pebbled Path. Privately, she realized she felt a bit better now that Pareal was gone. She felt freer and lighter than she had before she met the strange creature; she was glad it was time to go.

Still, a tiny question lingered at the back of her mind, had she really just seen a friend, or had she brushed against trouble in disguise?

Her thoughts were bombarded by the striking beauty of the land. Peeville was beautiful. It was the fragrances of the countryside that made her heart swell. She inhaled deeply, both the sights and the smells. The aroma in the air seemed to swirl around her head. It was sweet and earthy. It really was a beautiful day.

MaPOP continued her pilgrimage with a dance and a song. She nodded to polite pink butterflies as they fluttered along. MaPOP looked around and said to herself, *I can hardly believe this day, it has been the best.*

MaPOP felt confused as she reflected on meeting Pareal. She thought to herself, *Who was that?* Further, she wondered, *Why would the Prince and Princess of the fabulous Purple Palace send me outdated information, special delivery?* Scrunching her face, she told herself, *It does not make sense.*

MaPOP thought further and asked herself why she was doubting her very credible information from the Prince and Princess themselves. She considered further why she had even believed the testimony of a strange creature at all. As MaPOP quickened her pace, she thought to herself, *What did the creature say its name was?* Then she recalled what it said. *It said its name was "Pareal."*

At that very moment, MaPOP decided with conviction: she was going to stay on the Pebbled Path, as directed by the fancy invitation to dinner from the Prince and Princess of the Purple Palace.

With her decision firm in her heart, MaPOP reached into her pocket to feel the gifts once more, the compass and the pocket watch. They were her guides, her treasures, her reminders that the Purple Palace awaited her. The steady ticking and unwavering needle assured her that she was on course. The day was still young, and her path was lit with promise.

CHAPTER 4

THE PUMPKIN AND PERSIMMON PATCH

MaPOP checked the time on the pocket watch gifted to her yesterday, along with many other gifts. Everything had arrived via special delivery, including the invitation to dinner at the Purple Palace with the Prince and Princess. She admired the pocket watch in her puppet hand. She marveled at the exquisite piece of jewelry. The face of her pocket watch told her it was 11:00 a.m.

It was very important to watch the time, to be on time. The invitation inside the beautifully decorated and bejeweled box had stated, *"Please arrive promptly at 7:00 p.m."*

MaPOP used her compass to confirm she was headed in the right direction. Her compass was also gifted by the Palace. It was every bit as stunning in beauty as the pocket watch. The compass had one letter on it, a decorative "P." She observed the whole perimeter of the compass was encircled by two rings of semi-precious stones: amethyst and peridot.

After assuring herself she was traveling in the right direction, she slid the compass back in the other pocket. She kept moving until she came upon a sign that read:

"Pumpkin and Persimmon Patch", with an arrow pointing in the direction she was headed.

MaPOP remembered the directions on the map indicating the next signpost was indeed the Pumpkin and Persimmon Patch. As she moved along in the direction advised by the sign, once again her thoughts returned to the creature Pareal. *What kind of name is Pareal?*

Immediately, she started to laugh at herself. She thought, *What kind of name is MaPOP?*

Her giggles bounced off the air around her, mixing with the crisp countryside breeze. Even though doubts had tugged at her earlier, her joy and determination carried her forward, step by step, closer to her magical destination.

She continued to ponder the strange encounter. In her puppet mind, she revisited the details. *He said he was going to the Palace. But why did he say the Pebbled Path was damaged? How could he know more than the staff at the Purple Palace?*

MaPOP continued in her private thoughts until she thought she heard the faint sound of piccolos and percussion instruments. The music was inviting, like a call on the wind, and MaPOP increased her pace.

MaPOP was moving closer to the Pumpkin and Persimmon Patch. As she walked further, she saw the grandest Pumpkin and Persimmon Patch she had ever seen.

There were pumpkins of every size and every color. There were pumpkins of every type: plaid pumpkins, tiny pumpkins, square pumpkins, long pumpkins, pumpkins on picks, hard pumpkins, pleather pumpkins, velvet pumpkins, giant pumpkins, blue pumpkins, prickly pumpkins, spotted pumpkins, and flat pumpkins.

Some of the pumpkins were so large they could be made into a house. Some of the pumpkins were so small it was very easy to step on them and never even notice.

The sight filled her eyes with wonder, an endless field of imagination, where every pumpkin seemed more peculiar than the last.

As she approached, the music got louder and louder. MaPOP's heart began to pound harder and harder.

There in the middle of the farm was a gigantic octagon-shaped tent with purple ribbons flying high all around. The ribbons seemed to pulsate and sway to the beat.

MaPOP looked in amazement and began to pick up her feet. Just as she reached the threshold of the tent, MaPOP knew she was about to see something she would never forget.

The air itself seemed to hold its breath, waiting for MaPOP to step inside.

When MaPOP reached the place where the music was made, she jumped up and down and started to scream. What MaPOP saw, she could not believe.

She saw penguins playing piccolos while they stamped their feet. Next to the penguins was a purple python snake. It swirled around in circles, making perfect figure eights. She saw polar bears picking petunias and pansies. Carefully, they wove wreaths and tossed them to those who passed by.

She saw a host of happy woodland creatures dancing around. They were popping purple popcorn and roasting giant hotdogs.

Everywhere she turned, the farm was alive with rhythm, laughter, and color.

They all wore wreaths while they sang a woodland song. And just when she thought there was nothing left to see, she saw two striped pumpkins prancing by, singing, *"twee-de-da-lee-dee."*

MaPOP looked around and, without a sound, she jumped on a piglet who ran around the farm. MaPOP held on tightly and thought to herself, *"I never imagined how much fun could be had."*

As her piglet ran around and she bounced up and down, she enjoyed the piccolo players' great sound. She wiggled and giggled to the pounding beats:

"boom-dah-dah-boom, boom-dah-dah-boom."

She really loved the rhythmic, sassy percussion sound.

When she looked up, she started to laugh at the pigeons in the air, all wearing crowns. As they flew around the top of the tent, they cooed, dropping gumdrops and candies everywhere they flew.

Just then, out of the corner of her eye, she saw movement. Someone was waving to tell her "hi." MaPOP waved back at the small figurine.

It was a small pink bunny wearing a purple beanie. MaPOP waved again, taking in the sight.

"What a cute little bunny," she thought. "I wonder what she wants."

When MaPOP reached the bunny, she hopped off the piglet. The piglet grunted a "see ya later" and scurried away.

The bunny motioned for MaPOP to follow. The bunny, wearing the purple beanie, moved to a corner and away from the crowd. MaPOP followed.

The bunny introduced herself as Agent Stanley.

When MaPOP introduced herself, she was surprised when the bunny said, *"I know who you are."*

The bunny handed her a purple package and told her not to open it until after her dinner at the Palace. MaPOP looked at the small package, a bit perplexed. She smiled to herself, then looked back to ask questions to Agent Stanley.

But to MaPOP's great surprise, Agent Stanley was gone, without a sound.

If MaPOP did not have the package in her hand, she would not have believed it happened. No, she did not understand. She tucked the small package into her backpack, then swirled around thinking about what had just happened.

The party in the Patch of the Pumpkins and Persimmons was so hearty, so grand, that, except for the mysterious Agent Stanley, no one else ever noticed MaPOP was even around.

As MaPOP made her way back to the entrance of the tent, she gently rubbed the piglet on its head and said goodbye. The piano and piccolos were playing loudly as she waved farewell.

The party was still hearty; no one noticed or cried as MaPOP walked away. There were no tears in their eyes.

MaPOP thought to herself she had a good time. It was just as much fun as when she visited Platesville town.

Now, moving onward and returning to the Pebbled Path, she chuckled to herself. While glad to be moving on the Pebbled Path again, she thought, *I know tomorrow those Pumpkins and Persimmons folks will be at it again.*

With a smile on her face and a mysterious new package in her pack, MaPOP's journey pressed on, full of wonder, full of questions, and still guided by the promise of the Purple Palace.

MaPOP refocused on the road ahead of her. Her thoughts wandered as she walked. With each step, she became more and more aware of the pebbles that made up the path. The pebbles were different colors and different sizes too. Each had been pressed deep into the earth, making the path smooth and easy to walk on.

Her eyes focused on the shape of each small stone. Then she halted abruptly. Instead of seeing more pebbles ahead, she was now focused on a pair of pointed, prickly toes.

MaPOP was perplexed and quickly followed the line up to the legs, tummy, face, and hair. It was Pareal, and MaPOP was greatly surprised again. She jumped back a bit to take this sight all in.

MaPOP looked at Pareal as he started to grin. This time MaPOP remained quiet. She studied his face as if she were going to paint his portrait. Her puppet eyes traced every line of his curved face, taking inventory of all the pimples scattered across it.

MaPOP said privately to herself, *"There is something quite peculiar about this thing."* Yes, there was something even stranger than his prickly toes and pimply face, "This creature, Pareal keeps appearing and disappearing. He seemed to pop up right in my face."

MaPOP said to Pareal, "I did not see or hear you approaching! Where did you come from?"

She looked to the left and then to the right, as if searching for the answer to her own question. She took a slow panoramic visual scan of the entire area. MaPOP saw nothing that suggested where he had been before he was suddenly standing in front of her.

She asked Pareal, "What are you doing here? And why didn't you say something? You startled me."

Her words hung in the air, but the Pebbled Path gave no answers, only Pareal's unsettling grin remained.

Pareal paused before he answered her. In this moment, he felt powerful, thinking MaPOP believed his intentions were pure. He thought to himself, *She thinks I will tell her the truth.*

Pareal smiled deceptively at MaPOP. Then he said in what he thought was an innocent voice, "Why are you pondering these things about me? I just met you about two hours ago. Just where do you think I should be?"

He said this to suggest she had no reason at all to think badly of him. Then he went on to explain, "I told you earlier, I had a few things to pack before I headed to the Palace. Now, about that?"

As if to prove his innocence, he held up a travel bag. He quickly winked an *"I told you so"* at MaPOP and pivoted. Without much thought, MaPOP started following. They began walking together on the Pebbled Path. Pareal looked over and told MaPOP, "You are as fickle as a pickle."

Pareal suggested they start moving faster, explaining that the Pebbled Path stretched on for miles and miles. Then, as if it were completely natural, as if he truly cared, Pareal asked MaPOP "What is the time?"

Before she realized it, MaPOP slipped her hand into her puppet pocket and pulled out the pocket watch. She told him, "The time is 11:49 a.m."

Pareal's jealous, envious eyes grew larger and larger as he watched the sunlight dance across the polished surface of the pocket watch. The rays swirled and flashed off the semi-precious stones encircling its golden face. He hated seeing her put the pocket watch away.

They continued their pilgrimage to the Palace as travel companions. Pareal made MaPOP laugh with his silly jokes, and even tried to dance, which made her giggle even more. Later, they walked quietly, each lost in private thoughts.

As they moved along, the synchronized calls of parrots to parakeets echoed high above in the sky. Pale white pigeons circled overhead, swooping gently past their heads before flying on.

MaPOP experienced great pleasure from the day's excitement and the profusion of beauty that surrounded them both as they made their way to the Purple Palace. In her private thoughts, she reasoned with herself. Even though Pareal made her laugh, she still felt something was not quite right about him.

For example, MaPOP wondered, *Why did Pareal not have his own pocket watch?* MaPOP thought, Surely, if I received a pocket watch in my special delivery present, Pareal should have received one as well.

She quickly interrupted her own thoughts, refusing to let doubt steal her joy. She told herself, "I will not worry or be anxious on such a wonder-filled day." To shake off the uneasiness, MaPOP broke the silence with an unexpected declaration. Jubilantly, she exclaimed, "I am going to the Purple Palace!"

She said these words with the same enthusiasm she had when she first saw the invitation to the Palace.

Her surprise declaration jolted Pareal from his private thoughts and back to the present moment. In truth, Pareal had been secretly organizing his wicked plan. In his heart, he schemed to misdirect MaPOP from the Pebbled Path, with one clear goal: to postpone her arrival at the Purple Palace.

If he did this she would not arrive promptly at 7:00 p.m., as the invitation requested. Pareal thought this was an excellent plan. He was not planning to hurt her physically, he just wanted to ruin her time. And, he wanted to interrupt the extravagant dinner at the Purple Palace with her late arrival. Pareal grinned because he really liked his plan.

At that very moment, the sun's golden rays pierced through the thick canopy of foliage created by the tall trees on both sides of the Pebbled Path. The two travelers paused briefly, smiling with delight as the light shimmered all around them.

The powerful beams danced upon MaPOP's precious purple pearls, scattering prisms of color all around them. It was as though the forest itself had joined in the celebration, wrapping them in a rainbow of living light.

Without warning, the sun rays were flashing purple rainbows of color everywhere. This sight almost blinded Pareal. The sight made MaPOP giggle with delight. The pearls were exquisite. MaPOP watched his reaction to the sunlight being reflected off the surface of the pearls. Pareal partially joked and said, "Your jewels are practically blinding me." He continued, "With so much light in my eyes I could get turned round and lose my way."

Pareal was not blinded by the light. He was blinded by his jealousy because he did not receive a special delivery present containing not only precious purple pearls, but he also missed out on the purple potted plant, the purple bubble wand, the plaid puppies, the purple shiny pieces, the weapon of prayer, the one-of-a-kind invitation (which he would have placed on his wall), or any of the other special gifts in the big purple "P" shaped box prepared and presented by the Purple Palace's royal staff.

MaPOP thought to herself quietly as she continued walking. MaPOP wondered, what did he mean when he said he could get lost? She watched Pareal. She was curious to see his reaction to her next question. Using a carefree voice she questioned Pareal, "How can you get lost on the Pebbled Path?" Pareal did not answer; he just made a funny face to acknowledge he heard her. They continued walking in silence. Quietly MaPOP asked herself, "Where is his compass, his pocket watch, and his pearls?"

A gentle breeze blew through the trees, forcing the sunlight away from the pearls. Again, MaPOP explored her growing suspicion that Pareal was strange. As the two pilgrims made their way towards the Purple Palace, the next signpost, based on the map, was the town of Ping2thePong.

As they kept walking, MaPOP asked Pareal "If he had visited the town of Ping2thePong before?" Pareal replied, "Yes, of course, they are just like family." MaPOP probed further, asking "What the residents were like." That's when a smile made its way all the way across Pareal's strange face. He said, "I think you will find them curious, like all the other residents in the land of the Purple Palace." He laughed, making eye contact with MaPOP. He continued laughing and said, "They will sandwich you with their very own special Ping2thePong welcome."

MaPOP replied, laughing, "Are they going to try and eat me?" "No, you fickle pickle," Pareal said. Then he followed with the strange statement, "You will see for yourself, MaPOP; you will see."

The two traveled further down the Pebbled Path toward the town of Ping2thePong. MaPOP traveled with Pareal believing he wanted what she wanted. MaPOP wanted to arrive at the Purple

Palace no later than 7:00 p.m. Pareal wanted to make MaPOP late for her arrival.

MaPOP observed the sun was in a different position in the sky. She began to move faster.

Her puppet heart filled with determination, she quickened her stride, knowing each step brought her closer not just to the curious town of Ping2thePong, but also one step nearer to the grand moment she longed for, her arrival at the Purple Palace.

CHAPTER 5

THE TOWN OF PING2THEPONG

Pong
Ping

MaPOP enjoyed the warm breeze and sunlight of the afternoon sun. She pondered the day's activities again. "Wow," she thought to herself, "the excitement leading to the pinnacle of my highest hopes in my puppet life could not be better." MaPOP thought, even though she had two incredible adventures in Platesville and the town of Pumpkin and Persimmon Patch, she suspected the joy and grandeur of the Purple Palace would eclipse her current sense of satisfaction.

Refocusing on the purpose of her travel, her thoughts drifted far away from both the towns she had visited that morning and Pareal. As she walked along the Pebbled Path, she imagined what the Purple Palace would be like up close. She recalled seeing the palace once before, far away from her home.

Her imaginative thoughts continued. Perhaps there were purple pillars holding up a canopy of fragrant flowers and creeping vines. She thought to herself, the canopy and vines held up by the purple pillars are woven together creating a unique tapestry of fragrances and colors.

In her mind, she could see, and almost smell, the sweet aroma of gardenias, jasmine, roses, freesia, hydrangeas, lavender, carnations, ivy, and philodendron. She imagined, as she walked on autopilot, that the flowers and vines were interwoven with the prettiest silk ribbons her puppet eyes had ever seen. The metallic silk ribbons reflected the sunlight so brightly that the canopy could be seen from miles away.

She imagined the royal staff's clothing as well. Not only did they have big welcoming smiles, but they wore short coats with large silver buttons. Their shirts were made from shiny taffeta, and their charcoal gray velvet slacks matched their gloves. In her imagination, both the male and female staff were equally stunning, every detail fit for royalty.

Just then, she remembered she had been instructed to ask for Pewter the moment she arrived.

Pretending she was already there, she corrected her posture and raised her puppet chin. She walked with confidence, pretending to hold up the skirt made of layers of lace and taffeta decorating her purple velvet gown with a high collar. She pretended to nod polite hello's to the other guests as she was led to her seat at the same table where the Prince and Princess were seated. Pretending the staff pulled out a chair and directed her to have a seat, she admired the elegant table, the centerpiece, the candles, and the fine China encrusted with jewels.

When she sat down, she imagined the priceless fabrics on the walls of the Purple Palace, its furniture, the royal attendants, and the other royal guests. Her imagination painted the tablecloths, the fine China, and the flatware, all decorated with lavender, periwinkle, red-violets, blue-violets, pastel purples, velvets, silks, and embroidered pillows, each piece in rich jewel-toned colors and textures to prove the nobility of the Prince and Princess.

MaPOP was about to imagine the palace grounds and its artwork when her daydream was abruptly invaded by the sound of Pareal's voice calling her name.

"Oh, Pareal!" MaPOP giggled as she returned to reality. She was still smiling about her creative imaginings. She stopped in her puppet footsteps. "Pareal, you called my name?"

MaPOP focused on Pareal, quickly studying him from the top of his pimply head to the pointed, prickly toes crawling out the tops of his shoes. Pareal was already staring at her, but this time he was pointing to a sign.

She read the sign and began to smile. Then she looked back in Pareal's direction, only to see he had already taken about ten steps away from her and off the Pebbled Path. To her surprise, one of his feet was already buried deep in the thick foliage just beyond the path's edge.

MaPOP asked, confusion in her voice, "You wanted me to see the sign?" She smiled faintly, still puzzled. "Ok."

MaPOP understood that after the town they were now approaching, there was only one more stop before the Purple Palace. The sign stood tall and clear, pointing the way: *This way to the town of Ping2thePong.*

Just then, Pareal calls MaPOP's name over his shoulder as he walks, or almost runs, into the forest. He says, "Catch up with you later in town. Be sure to arrive before 2:00; the Pings and the Pongs play their favorite game every day at the same time." He finished with, "It's quite a spectacle." He slows, then turns and smiles a strange smile, then says, "I know a few people in this part of the kingdom. I will see you around."

MaPOP thought two different things. She could not decide which thought came first. One thought was, "Good riddance to ya, Pareal." Something about Pareal made her uncomfortable. The second thought was her wondering, *What kind of town names itself Ping2thePong?*

MaPOP continued on the Pebbled Path. As she was walking, she decided to check the time. She wanted to keep up with the time because she did not want to be late. She reached deep inside her pants pocket. Inside was her priceless pocket watch gifted by the Prince and Princess of the Purple Palace. MaPOP valued this prized, priceless possession. The time was 1:49 p.m.

A few moments passed as MaPOP walked in silence. MaPOP entered the town of Ping2thePong. She did not receive a warm or a cold greeting from the residents of this strange town. She did not receive a welcome at all. The silence felt unusual compared to the lively greetings she had expected.

It was strange to MaPOP because there was only one large building with one large doorway. But she did immediately understand the name of the town. Everywhere she looked there were large brown balls; they looked like giant ping pong balls. She kept walking straight ahead. Then she saw a sign painted on the wall. MaPOP noticed the wet paint on the sign was dripping, as though someone was working very fast and not paying attention to the details. The sign read, "Visitors This Way."

The arrow on the sign directed MaPOP to another narrow corridor. MaPOP heard something that sounded like cheering.

Five minutes had passed as she walked further. MaPOP was forced to enter a corridor that was even smaller than the previous passage. Additionally, she recognized the passageway had become almost pitch black. However, there was a bright light ahead of her, so she was not worried about falling on her puppet face. MaPOP felt a little anxious. "What is going on?" she wondered to herself.

With each puppet step, she could see a bright light and hear the sounds of a large crowd. The sounds appeared to be a combination of unorganized chants, chides, and cheers. Walking closer to the bright light, she could make out two words of the chants: *Ping* and *Pong*. It was a rhythmic chant. It sounded as though a group of Pings were chanting their name. Then the Pongs would follow in rhythm.

MaPOP reached the bright lights. As she stepped into the space where all the commotion was taking place, her mind was catapulted into puppet shock. On the other side of the large circular room, way up high, she saw Pareal on a patio with several other ping pong balls.

MaPOP immediately knew something was not right. The chanting, Pareal on the patio, and the narrow passageway each individually raised a flag of concern. She decided to walk further into the narrowing passageway, moving up a ramp or an elevation. Finally, she stopped at a glass door. Again, MaPOP felt uncomfortable, as if something unpleasant was about to happen. She did not try to open the door right away. She stood and listened as the noisemakers were settling down.

MaPOP listened and noticed balls were rolling away from the center of the room. She understood she was in some sort of arena. Directly in front of her was a net that divided the space into two equal parts. Her puppet heart beat faster as she wondered if she was about to witness a game, or be pulled into one.

From her position at the top of the ramp behind the glass door, she could see the patio where she had seen Pareal very well. One of the giant brown ping pong balls used his hands and arms to signal to the crowd to calm down. Another giant ping pong ball with a golden crown twirled forward to a podium. She greeted the pavilion of brown balls warmly. Then, to MaPOP's great surprise, she motioned by waving her hand for Pareal to come forward. The crowd of brown ping pong balls cheered. Then they quieted down.

As MaPOP listened, it was clear to her Pareal had provided special entertainment for the Ping2thePong community. He asked a ping pong ball to come over and stand by him. Then he looked to the crowd of ping pong balls and shouted valiantly, "Let the games begin!" The crowd cheered, shouting in response to the crowned ball's command. The brown ball Pareal had invited to join him on the elevated patio twirled forward. The crowd erupted in excited screams. The brown ball allowed Pareal to pin a sign to his back and one to his front. The back sign read *Pongs* and the front sign read *Pings*. Two other brown balls rolled forward. They began to spin the ball around and around. When the ball stopped spinning, the sign that read *Pings* was facing the crowned ball. The crowd cheered!!!

MaPOP continued to be perplexed, trying to understand what was going on. She decided to push the door open just enough to see what these giant brown ping pong balls were up to. There was so much commotion she was not concerned that someone would see her. She peeked her puppet head around the door and noticed two rows of brown balls playing snare drums, marching her way in formation.

Just then, she heard a ruckus behind her. She stepped to the side just in time for 25–30 brown balls with purple and white polka dot helmets on their heads. She looked across the arena on the opposite side of the net and saw a similar sight, except the approaching balls wore white helmets with purple polka dots. The arena pulsed with energy, the chants of "Ping" and "Pong" growing louder as if the walls themselves were echoing their rhythm.

It was 01:58 p.m.

MaPOP studied the situation. She thought to her puppet self, they are about to play a game like ping pong. MaPOP observed that all the Pings were on one side of the pavilion. *I guess they will be moving some object back and forth,* but she could not figure out where or what it was.

Just then, just like at the town of the Pumpkins and Persimmon Patch, her peripheral vision detected movement. She looked closer. It was that little bunny wearing the purple beanie, Agent Stanley. She motioned for MaPOP to get down low to the ground. Intuitively, MaPOP bent her puppet knees and squinted her face as if asking for more information.

Just then, a large whistle was blown by somebody and suddenly MaPOP understood what Ping2thePong meant. The balls were hurling themselves across the arena and over the net MaPOP was kneeling under. MaPOP wondered how she would get out of this volatile ping pong game. She glanced back in the direction where she last saw Agent Stanley. Agent Stanley had moved. Now she was directly in front of MaPOP, at the other end of the net.

"Run!" Agent Stanley screamed.

"What?" MaPOP responded.

"Run now, as fast as you can!" Agent Stanley shouted back. She had a big voice for such a small bunny.

Suddenly, as if she were transformed into a race car, MaPOP began running across the arena in front of the ping pong net at full speed. She had run a third of the way before both the Pings and Pongs audiences started cheering loudly. They were actually laughing and clapping.

As MaPOP kept running, the Pings and Pongs on the playing field reacted to the crowds. Both groups searched the room to understand the commotion. They spotted MaPOP running low, full speed across their arena. Now alerted to her movements, one of the Pongs decided to charge her. It spun around and around, then accelerated forward, trying to anticipate the best place to bounce into the net. The crowd cheered. Not to be outdone, a Ping responded in turn.

The arena suddenly became chaotic, the chants of "Ping!" and "Pong!" thundering louder as the players turned their attention from the game to MaPOP. What had once been a match was now a chase, and the puppet found herself at the very center of the spectacle.

Agent Stanley guided MaPOP through the ping pong nightmare. Just as MaPOP was almost clear of the physical trauma of colliding with a giant brown ball, she heard the crowd cheering louder and louder. If she did not know better, she could almost believe the crowd was cheering for her. She lifted her head just a bit for any final instructions from Agent Stanley. Agent Stanley's face was distorted with an imminent-danger worried look. Then, out of nowhere, she saw that she was going to meet the full force of a Ping and a Pong. Wham, smash, then puppet sandwich!

The crowd roared their approval loudly. Each of the balls, undamaged, took bows and rolled their way back to their respective teams. After swerving to the left at full speed, MaPOP learned she did not have the agility to avoid the well-timed contact. The crowd in the pavilion roared with excitement once more. As MaPOP proclaimed her discomfort with a loud *"Ouch!"* Agent Stanley came to her aid. She motioned for MaPOP to follow her. The ping pong games continued.

Though sore and shaken, MaPOP managed to keep moving, following Agent Stanley step for step. Each roar of the crowd behind her only reminded her how close she had come to being trapped inside that strange game forever.

The cheers of the crowd were becoming faint as they moved further and further away from the pavilion, arena, and the town of Ping2thePong. The sun was approaching the horizon. There were so many thoughts swirling in MaPOP's mind about what had just happened. When Agent Stanley confirmed MaPOP was okay, she excused herself, explaining she had to be on her way.

When she stepped on the Pebbled Path again, she really was not sure which direction led to the Palace and which direction would take her home. She reached her puppet hand deep into the other pocket and retrieved the compass. Like the pocket watch, the compass was an extravagant piece of art. The Mother of Pearl face of the compass had one arrow and one letter. The letter "P" was in the "north" position. The special instructions included in the special delivery package indicated the dial on the compass would always point to the Purple Palace.

She placed the compass in her hand. She turned first to the left, watching the needle's movement. Then she turned to the right. When she turned to the right, the dial of the compass moved away from the letter "P." The compass answered her question about which way to go after returning to the Pebbled Path.

MaPOP faced left and began walking at a brisk pace. She did not want to think about the recent visit. She freed her mind and enjoyed the scenery. She sighed, a bit exhausted from being made into a ping pong puppet sandwich. She was confident the experience was the first and the last.

With the compass guiding her and the sun dipping low, MaPOP pressed onward, her thoughts fixed on the Purple Palace and the promise of what lay ahead.

MaPOP walked quietly with her backpack. She touched the pearls around her neck. She was so happy there was one final stop on her way to the Purple Palace for dinner at 7:00 p.m. She looked up at the sky as she walked. MaPOP attempted to see recognizable shapes among the cloud formations. When that began to bore her, she created a new game to keep her mind occupied. She began to study the various sizes of the pebbles embedded firmly in the Pebbled Path. She made note of the colors and sizes of the stones. As she walked, she wondered where all the pebbles came from. She thought she saw a pattern in the placement of the pebbles making up the path. She concluded the placements did appear random, but there was definitely a pattern.

She continued studying the pebbles until her view of the path was blocked by a pair of peculiar, prickly, pointed toes falling out of a pair of shoes sprinkled with paint splatter.

MaPOP followed the line leading from the shoes to the face of the creature who wore them. It was Pareal!! MaPOP did not slow her pace; she simply walked around him and focused her eyes on the horizon. Pareal pivoted to follow her. He called out, "MaPOP, MaPOP slow down," he pleaded. "Where are your manners?" he asked. "You did not greet me." Pareal sped up, realizing she was not slowing down.

Now walking beside MaPOP, Pareal asked, "MaPOP, what is your hurry?" He pleaded for her to slow down. MaPOP pushed her hands into her pocket and proceeded at the same pace. Pareal was frustrated. He did not know what to do. He decided not to bring up their visit to the town of Ping2thePong. He decided he would just savor his collection of memories of MaPOP running through the narrow passageway privately. He felt happy about the silly prank he orchestrated. He rationalized that MaPOP had not been hurt or damaged. He concluded, wrongly, that there was no real harm caused by his prank of making MaPOP the special entertainment.

But deep down, MaPOP could feel the air shift. Something about Pareal's presence no longer felt like a harmless prank, it felt heavier, almost foreboding. She pressed on, determined not to let him slow her down.

They walked in silence. MaPOP could not forget having to run as fast as she could to avoid getting pummeled by giant ping pong balls. Pareal was privately reviewing the details of the next step in his plan to redirect MaPOP. He was such a pitiful creature. He still wanted to make MaPOP arrive late for dinner at the Purple Palace. He was still jealous and envious that MaPOP received a special delivery package from the Prince and Princess of the Purple Palace and he did not. He was disturbed; he did not receive the gifts given to her: a potted plant nested in a fragrant pile of purple petals, a purple flute that released purple iridescent bubbles that faded into letter "P's" as they disappeared, the two plaid poodle puppies, the shiny things in a plastic purple pouch, the purple pearls, the weapon of prayer, and the special instructions containing the invitation to dinner at the Purple Palace. No, Pareal was not given any of these gifts by the Prince and Princess.

Finally, Pareal interrupted the silence of their pilgrimage. "MaPOP," he began. "We are almost at the Purple Palace. You may remember I told you the Pebbled Path had been damaged? Well, there is a detour just before the Potato Pits." MaPOP just kept walking in silence. She did not believe this creature to be a true friend or even a nice person. Therefore, she suspected everything he said was a lie or only partially true. Since MaPOP was not interested in engaging Pareal, he decided he would slip away quietly to enact the last terrible plan he had up his prickly sleeves.

Fifteen minutes passed before MaPOP recognized she was walking alone. When she realized Pareal had disappeared again, she shook her head from left to right. She braced herself for what was to come. She knew Pareal was not to be trusted. She continued to walk past meadows and plains. The woodland creatures seemed to wave hello as she passed by. Then she looked far up the path. It looked like Pareal. He was very far up the path, and MaPOP wondered what shortcut he had taken to get so far ahead of her. Again, she wondered what he was up to now. MaPOP kept walking on the Pebbled Path until she reached Pareal.

Her pace slowed as she realized the signposts ahead were shifting, pointing her toward the next mysterious place, the Potato Pits. MaPOP took a deep breath, readying herself. Whatever waited there, she knew it would mark the next chapter of her journey.

CHAPTER 6
THE POTATO PITS

Potatoe Pits
Royal Detour

MaPOP wondered with some reservation what she would encounter at the town called Potato Pits. She reflected on the day's events. She recalled she had left her home before the sunlight kissed the morning sky. MaPOP was traveling on the Pebbled Path with fresh excitement.

She smiled as she recalled the warmth of the sun and the odor of fertilized fields. She recalled each beautiful detail of the amazing start of her pilgrimage. She remembered arriving at the Pebbled Path. She remembered the chirping voices of the birds floating on the morning dew. She remembered the earthy smell in the morning air.

MaPOP was exhilarated thinking about how far she had come. She thought about the fabulous voices of the "singing" Plates at Platesville. She thought about the commotion and excitement at the Pumpkin Persimmon Patch. She thought about the unexpected encounter with the bunny in the purple beanie. She even pondered the likeability of the creature Pareal. She was not fond of him. MaPOP thought he just seemed creepy and untrustworthy. She recalled he had not really done anything to her, with the one exception of featuring her as the special entertainment at the town of Ping2thePong.

Even so, something in her puppet heart whispered that his intentions were far from pure. She could not explain why, but she felt uneasy whenever his prickly presence was near.

MaPOP did not know Pareal was just getting warmed up with his plan to make her arrive late to the Purple Palace.

Pareal's jealousy of MaPOP grew with each passing moment. He was jealous. He was envious. He was angry. This made him very petty in his thinking and behavior. Pareal was thinking it was time to put his plan into action. He just wanted to delay her arrival to the royal Purple Palace.

Little did MaPOP realize that as she moved closer to the Potato Pits, Pareal's mischievous schemes were already taking shape. The smooth Pebbled Path ahead was about to twist into yet another trial.

Pareal had a pouch with him that held his tools of deception. These were the tools he planned to use to create a reason for MaPOP to trust him. Inside his pouch were paint and brushes. His plan involved painting a second Pebbled Path and a second sign. It was Pareal that painted the sign of deception at the town of Ping2thePong. MaPOP noticed the dripping paint on the sign directing "visitors" (her) into the narrow passageway under the net in the Ping2thePong arena. His next and final move was to trick MaPOP from the right path to the wrong path. He had to get busy because he was running out of time. He had underestimated the little puppet's determination and drive. She was indeed a formidable foe.

MaPOP continued to ponder the strange inhabitants of Ping2thePong and their fierce game of ping pong. Getting sandwiched at the last minute was not fun to her, even though she chuckled as she remembered how the crowd roared with excitement. The two giant brown balls with helmets that collided with her were true gladiators. It was not fun. Then she asked herself why Pareal was there. Why didn't he join her when she arrived? MaPOP concluded he was some type of phony. She decided right then to be cautious of everything he said moving forward.

Her puppet heart resolved to be wiser from this point on. The journey was no longer just about reaching the Purple Palace, it was about guarding herself against deception and staying on the Pebbled Path.

With renewed confidence, MaPOP pushed onward on the Pebbled Path. She checked the time again. MaPOP started jogging. She had fifty-seven minutes to arrive on time. She thought to herself, *Purple Palace, here I come.*

Her advancement up the hill to the Palace gave her a spectacular panoramic view of the entire valley. This was just one of the many valleys in the kingdom of the Purple Palace. It was absolutely stunning, the trees, shrubs, crystal clear water, the purple mist waterfalls, snow-crested mountains, woodland animals, birds, and of course the Palace.

MaPOP could not see the Purple Palace from her position, but she knew it was every bit as fabulous. She jogged in silence, pondering all the day's activities.

And though the road ahead was uncertain, she felt her determination burning brighter than ever, one step closer to the Purple Palace, and one step farther from Pareal's schemes.

Pareal was busy painting his fake Pebbled Path. He knew MaPOP would reach this part of the real Pebbled Path soon. Pareal did not know MaPOP had started jogging. Pareal had not brought a drop cloth to catch the paint splatter. He was moving fast, and there was quite a bit of splatter. As soon as he had painted the imposter Pebbled Path as far as his petty eyes could see, he felt strangely confident.

He moved his freshly splattered pointed prickly feet over to the signpost for the town of Potato Pits. The big arrow on the sign was covered with tiny potatoes on long vines. He quickly snatched all of the potatoes off the sign, tossing them haphazardly behind himself. Then, with sinister precision, he turned the arrow in the opposite direction. He did this so the arrow on the sign pointed towards the fake Pebbled Path. Pareal quickly gathered the paint and brushes. He pushed them, still full of paint, into his pouch. He then used the pouch as a towel to wipe the paint from his hands. He had forgotten soap.

After tossing the pouch into the bushes, Pareal leaned against a tree and sighed. His face was flushed and he was sweating. He took two or three more deep breaths. Just then, in the distance, he saw MaPOP approaching on the real Pebbled Path. Pareal smiled a sinister smile, showing all of his prickly teeth.

MaPOP was getting closer, but she did not see Pareal yet. She had stopped jogging. Now she was pirouetting her puppet self down the path. Even though she was spinning and looking like a tiny tornado, MaPOP did not feel dizzy. She felt great, brave, exhilarated, strong, and happy all at once. MaPOP replaced all the anxious thoughts in her puppet mind with creative speculation of the grandeur she would be immersed into as soon as she arrived at the Purple Palace.

As Pareal watched her dancing approach, he was thinking, *"Stop being so happy, MaPOP!"* Pareal began to mimic MaPOP's dancing and prancing about as if he were also happy. He stopped himself from his phony happiness dance and clumsy pirouettes. Catching his bad breath, Pareal refocused on his response to not being invited to the Purple Palace.

Pareal was petty. He could not be happy that MaPOP was invited and he was not. He was angry that MaPOP was given a special treat and he was not. He was envious MaPOP was gifted priceless treasures along with the personal invitation to the Purple Palace from the Prince and Princess. He wished it was him. But since it was not him, he was going to continue in his pettiness.

In his heart, bitterness grew heavier with every breath, while MaPOP's joy seemed to rise lighter with every step. Their paths, though side by side, could not have been more different.

MaPOP had lost count of the number of pirouettes she had executed. She was busy pirouetting her way to the Potato Pits and then to the Purple Palace. She stopped when she saw Pareal. They made eye contact. MaPOP said, "hello Pareal." Pareal was lost in thought, trying to determine the best way to manipulate MaPOP. MaPOP said it again, "hello Pareal."

As Pareal exited his private thoughts, he looked directly at MaPOP. He was standing in front of the real Pebbled Path. Behind him were branches he had dragged onto the real Pebbled Path. As long as MaPOP did not step behind him, his plan to deceive and delay her just might work.

Just then MaPOP noticed the paint splatter on his hands and feet. Her eyes returned to Pareal's. She noticed smudges of paint on his face as well. She immediately remembered the wet sign directing her to the entrance of the narrow passageway. MaPOP felt something was not right. She looked into Pareal's eyes. They did not give her any more information. MaPOP knew Pareal was up to something.

Something stirred deep inside her puppet soul, a warning, a quiet certainty that the creature Pareal meant to cause her trouble. She could not figure out exactly what he was up to. Then she remembered the special instructions about what to do in a circumstance like the one she was facing.

MaPOP pulled her backpack from her puppet shoulders. She unzipped a side pocket on the backpack and reached inside. She had placed a single item in the pocket of her backpack. She shivered a little as her hand felt the coolness of the metal object. She tightened her grasp of the item in the backpack.

It was the weapon of the prayer heart. Briefly, MaPOP wondered how a small metal heart could be an effective weapon with so much unknown. Securing the golden heart in her hand, she pulled her hand out of the backpack. She never took her gaze from Pareal's eyes as she retrieved the heart. She held the heart tightly, not knowing what to expect.

She remembered the instructions directed her to believe help was imminent. Just then MaPOP remembered her compass that always points to the Purple Palace.

With the heart in one hand and the compass in mind, she steadied herself. Something told her that this moment was a turning point, one that would test not just her courage, but her faith in the gifts she had been given.

Pareal spoke up. "MaPOP," he said. "You are almost there. You have made excellent time and are sure to arrive at the Palace on time." What Pareal said was true, but he was trying to flatter MaPOP. He was saying nice things to her that he really did not mean at all. Then he casually lifted his arm, pointing to the signpost for the Potato Pits. He was directing MaPOP in the wrong direction. Then, as if talking to a gullible creature, he said to MaPOP, "the rest of your journey is in the direction of the arrow." He thought he sounded very believable.

MaPOP was still clutching the weapon of prayer. She looked him up and down. She thought to herself, *why does he have so much paint on him?* She noticed further, he had a lot of fresh paint on his hands, clothes, and shoes. It was in that exact instant she saw the paint splatter marks on the arrow of the sign directing travelers to the Potato Pits.

Keeping her thoughts private, she pondered why the arrow would have paint on it. She wondered why the paint on the arrow was the same color as the fresh paint splatter on Pareal. MaPOP concluded Pareal had touched the arrow. But why would he touch the arrow, MaPOP wondered.

MaPOP began to move closer to Pareal. He seemed to be hiding something. Pareal froze where he stood. MaPOP was getting closer and closer, and he did not know what to do. Pareal backed up, asking MaPOP what she was doing. MaPOP responded, "Pareal, you seem fearful. What is going on?" MaPOP took another step closer.

Pareal backed up again, but this time he stumbled backwards into the branches he used to block MaPOP's view of the real Pebbled Path. His prickly feet went up into the air. As he fell backwards, branches scattered everywhere. His fall into the branches behind him exposed what he was trying to hide.

In that revealing moment, MaPOP's suspicions hardened into certainty. The truth was laid bare before her eyes, and the tangled deception Pareal had spun was now unraveling.

MaPOP looked at the 2nd Pebbled Path now in her view. MaPOP said Pareal's name very fast. "Pareal, what are you up to?" she said this loudly. She thought, *oh my, there are two pebble paths.* For a second, she felt confused and a bit anxious because it was getting very close to 7:00 p.m.

Just then she remembered the compass that was given to her. The compass would point her in the right direction to the Palace and the Potato Pits. She pulled it from her pocket and held it in front of her. First, she pointed it at the painted Pebbled Path. The needle on the compass moved away from the letter "P" on the face of the compass. Next, MaPOP positioned the compass directly in front of the real Pebbled Path. The needle on the face of the compass pointed directly to the letter "P".

MaPOP stepped over Pareal, who was still on the ground. She went back to the arrow on the signpost and turned it back to its true direction. Now she understood why the sign had wet paint on it. Then she looked over at Pareal. She did not have time for questions and answers with him. She felt a little sad because of the intended deception. She resumed the pilgrimage by herself.

Her heart beat faster with each step, not from fear, but from determination. She knew the Purple Palace was within her reach, and nothing Pareal did could hold her back now.

MaPOP took another 100 steps on the real Pebbled Path. Just ahead of her was a wreath of potatoes and potato vines. It was positioned by a large doorway at the base of a very large tree. MaPOP stepped inside the doorway. It was very dark, damp, very warm, and earthy.

After a few moments MaPOP's eyes adjusted to the darkness. She was inside something like a cave. She kept walking further into the dimly lit space. As she moved further she recognized the ground was slanted. She could tell with each step she was going further underground. It was very quiet. The space was lit by a dim purplish light. She did not know where it was coming from.

MaPOP walked and kept walking until she reached a strange door. It was covered with vines and roots. It looked very old. The ancient door had seven torches on both sides. The torches carried the same dim purple light. Collectively, they created a beautiful glow that felt safe to MaPOP.

Though deep underground, she sensed she was standing at the threshold of something mysterious and important, something that might bring her closer to the Purple Palace.

The underground door deep inside the Potato Pits cave had an extraordinary crystal handle. The handle, a type of doorknob, seemed to be older than the door itself. There was something magical, attractive, and inviting about the light reflected off the facets of the fine crystal. It seemed to glow.

MaPOP looked first to the right and then to the left. She was scanning her environment for any reason not to touch and turn the glowing crystal doorknob. Not seeing anyone or any reason not to, MaPOP did it.

When she touched and twisted the doorknob, nothing happened. So MaPOP pushed the door open; it was not heavy even though it was more than 20 feet tall. She stepped across the doorway, and the room began to spin. As the room spun, colors and light bounced all around her. It was a portal of some kind. Inside the portal MaPOP was tumbling around and around. She was also bouncing, going up and down.

MaPOP closed her puppet eyes for a second. The spinning and up-and-down movement began to take its toll on her equilibrium. When she opened her eyes again, MaPOP gently landed on the ground. She was out of the portal and very deep underground. The first thing she recognized were the hundreds, maybe thousands, of brown, white, and green vines, there were lots and lots of them. The vines were of different thicknesses. The light was different; it was brighter but it still had a purple glow.

As her eyes adjusted to the new light, she realized on each of the vines were all types of potatoes: sweet, white, yellow, purple, blue, red, and more. It was like stepping into a secret underground garden, alive with color and growth.

As she continued to survey her surroundings, MaPOP was interrupted by an unfamiliar sound. She turned in the direction of the sound. As she did this, a large potato rolled right in front of her and stopped. It stood straight up when it reached her. The big potato was covered with eyes all over it. Some of the eyes on the potato had begun to sprout tiny leaves. It was a giant sweet potato.

MaPOP blinked twice, unsure if she should laugh, run, or say hello. Something told her this strange potato was more than just a vegetable, it was alive, and it was waiting for her.

"Welcome MaPOP to the Potato Pits!" The deep, warm voice coming from the large potato continued, "we do not get many puppets passing through here."

Next, the large spud introduced himself as Pa. MaPOP smiled, wondering how he knew her name.

"Pa," she asked, "how do you know who I am?"

Pa chuckled. "We spuds have been expecting you. We know there is a dinner at the Purple Palace this evening, and we want to help you get there on time. The royal staff informed us."

He added quickly, "We are almost out of time. Come, let me give you a quick tour before you are on your way."

MaPOP walked next to him as he led the way to a huge cavern that was much deeper than MaPOP could see. There were many levels, and many of the levels were covered by thick vines which also continued deep down into the cavern. MaPOP realized that if she wanted, she could use the vines to climb down, deep, deep into the Potato Pit. It was actually a warm, earthy environment.

Then Pa said to MaPOP, "I want to introduce you to the Tater Tots. They have been practicing a dance called the *Tater Trot*, and they really want to perform it for you." The large spud chuckled heartily and motioned for MaPOP to follow.

MaPOP was intrigued by the dance of the tots; but she was also very concerned about the time. It was very important to her to arrive on time. Even though she was concerned about the time, she decided to follow the large spud. She did not want to be rude.

As she followed him, she could see a bright light and hear lots of percussion instruments. The pounding of the drums and the clanging of the cymbals was mesmerizing. MaPOP readjusted her eyes to the light and began to sway and walk at the same time. She chuckled to see hundreds of tater tots lining up to do their dance, the *Tater Trot*. They were dropping off the vines and moving into formation in an orderly way.

The ground beneath her seemed to pulse with the rhythm of their music, and MaPOP couldn't help but wonder what surprise awaited her in this strange and lively place.

The music quieted as the tots lined up with precision. There were hundreds of them. The vines moved back, creating a dance floor. MaPOP was giddy, she knew she would never forget this scene.

When every tot was in place, the light dimmed again. Then MaPOP heard a loud whistle and, to her surprise, the tater tots performed the best precision movements she had ever seen. Not one spud missed a beat. It was definitely worth seeing. Their entire dance, from beginning to end, lasted about three minutes. It was so cute! When they finished, as one united group, they bowed.

MaPOP clapped loudly; she wanted to stay longer, but she could not.

MaPOP checked her watch one last time. It was 6:49. MaPOP had only eleven minutes to arrive on time. She put the pocket watch back in her pocket. She felt sad because she thought she was going to arrive at the Purple Palace late. As the group completed their dance, Pa politely clapped and waited for the tots to exit. MaPOP moved over to the largest spud and explained her dilemma. She confided she had five minutes to arrive at the Purple Palace on time.

MaPOP talked with Pa, explaining she just could not be late. Pa nodded in understanding and pointed to a gate. MaPOP waved goodbye as she pranced away, hopeful that it was not too late. MaPOP got excited; she was ready to celebrate.

MaPOP pushed the gate and, to her surprise, she entered another portal filled with purple penguins. MaPOP was positive the penguins knew the way. They were like purple police to save the day. The portal kept spinning, sparking bright lights. MaPOP grabbed her puppet tummy as the spinning tickled her with delight. The penguins pushed a purple button and the portal door flew wide open.

MaPOP teared up when she stepped outside the portal. She could not believe her puppet eyes. The portal had delivered her right to the door of the grand Purple Palace, with servants galore.

The moment she had been waiting for had finally arrived…

MaPOP was now positioned for the best night of her puppet life. Pewter was waiting for her right by the door. The royal staff of the Purple Palace pampered her. When they finished, she felt refreshed. They curled her braids and pressed her clothes. Next, they painted MaPOP's fingernails and toes. Finally, they placed purple glitter lipstick on her lips. Then, to her surprise, they put her clothes, pressed and cleaned, back into her backpack.

MaPOP screamed when she saw the beautiful velvet gown she was to wear. It was decorated with embroidery, lace ribbon, and a high collar. She put it on quickly, checking her reflection in the floor-to-ceiling mirror. Next, they gave her a matching hat and purse that coordinated perfectly with the gown and the purple slippers she hurried to put on.

Her transformation was complete, and MaPOP hardly recognized the radiant figure looking back at her in the mirror.

All the guests had arrived. Pewter winked at MaPOP when he saw her gown. The staff led her to a grand ballroom where she waited for her turn to be led in. When it was her turn, she was escorted to the royal table. MaPOP had never seen such a fabulous display of finery and opulence, it took her breath away.

When the Prince and Princess arrived, MaPOP thought they were perfect. They both had purple hair pinned up in fancy letter "P"s. When they sat down at the table, they asked MaPOP about her trip to the Palace. They inquired if MaPOP had any difficulty. MaPOP shook her head no and offered information that a strange creature named Pareal had tried to trick her unsuccessfully. She refused to spoil the wonderful evening by thinking of anything unpleasant.

She reminded herself: this was a night for joy, gratitude, and celebration, not for shadows.

MaPOP thanked the Prince and Princess for the gifts and invitation. She told them she had never received anything like that large "P"-shaped box delivered by their staff. MaPOP thought it important to say thank you for each gift in detail.

MaPOP began by describing the splendor of the delivery man. She had never seen a purple hat and matching cape.

When MaPOP opened the large "P"-shaped box there were seven smaller boxes of assorted sizes. MaPOP continued:

1st – the potted plant with pansies, primrose, petunias, and philodendron, nestled in a profusion of purple flower petals.
2nd – the purple Flute releasing hypnotizing bubbles.
3rd – two pink and purple plaid poodles wearing sparkling pastel collars.
4th – plastic pouch containing a pound of shiny objects.
5th – a necklace of 24 precious purple pearls.
6th – weapon of prayer, a small golden heart.
7th – a box encrusted with jewels containing: invitation to dinner, compass, map, and the special instructions.

As MaPOP recited each treasure, her voice trembled with wonder, and the royal couple listened intently, their faces glowing with pride.

MaPOP thanked the Princess and Prince for the best two days of her puppet life. When dinner was over, MaPOP prepared to leave. The evening had been everything she imagined. She thanked them again for their extravagant hospitality. The Prince motioned to a staff member.

The staff member nodded and asked MaPOP to follow him. MaPOP followed the man without hesitation. The staffer took MaPOP's backpack and filled it with delectable treats. Next, he asked MaPOP to follow him.

Her heart felt full, her spirit light, and her gratitude immeasurable. Every detail of her journey had led her to this very moment.

MaPOP recognized she was leaving a different way than the way she arrived. She followed quietly, pleased with how the day turned out. She was pleased with everything, except Pareal. The goodbye from the royal staffer's mouth pulled MaPOP away from her private thoughts. He smiled and pointed to the purple crystal doorknob right next to his purple-gloved hand. He nodded, granting her authorization to touch the knob and turn it. Just like when MaPOP was in the Potato Pits, she touched the knob and turned it.

MaPOP remembers hearing POOF, PING, and POW. The next thing she knew, she was in front of her home. MaPOP shrugged her shoulders, thinking no one would believe what had just happened. She sighed with a sense of satisfaction. Looking up at the periwinkle blue sky, MaPOP knew she had just enjoyed an adventure.

She walked into the building and headed straight to her neighbor's home. She was anxious to play with the pink and purple plaid puppies. MaPOP smiled as she knocked on his door. She could hear her new puppies yelping.

But little did MaPOP know, endings often carry the seeds of new beginnings. The treasures she received, the invitation she accepted, and the adventures she faced were not merely a story to be finished, they were the foundation of something far greater still to come.

CHAPTER 7
THE PURPLE PALACE

MaPOP could not believe the day she had just experienced. It started yesterday afternoon with an ordinary knock on her door. Knock. Knock. Knock. After the knocking at her door, nothing was the same. She remembered hearing the warm, official-sounding voice she had never heard before announce a special delivery for MaPOP. As she reflected, she shook her puppet head from left to right slowly several times, as if thinking she still did not believe it.

Pewter was the name of the royal staff member who made the delivery to her home. He presented her with a large purple box in the shape of the letter "P." MaPOP thought to herself it was certainly a perplexing, exciting, and unforgettable presentation.

MaPOP reflected on how hard it was to contain her excitement when she left her home before the sun's rays began hiding the night sky. She revisited as many details as she could about the very first part of her journey: the smells, the crisp morning air, and the sounds of cows greeting each other. The two pastures she crossed were the last familiar places once she reached the Pebbled Path. She remembered she had stopped to rest a bit before venturing on her journey to the Purple Palace.

MaPOP remembered it did not take very long to reach the town of Platesville. It was her first landmark according to the map gifted to her by the Prince and Princess. She visited the home of the famous Prazin Plates and was ecstatic to enjoy the spontaneous performance. She was deeply moved by the experience and not only sang along, she also danced.

MaPOP learned about the party life at the town of Pumpkin and Persimmon Patch. The woodland animals and all their pals enjoyed music, food, and candy treats. In this town MaPOP met Agent Stanley for the first time. Agent Stanley was a tiny bunny who wore a purple beanie. She was a foot long from the tip of her floppy ears to her toes. She had given MaPOP a small package with the instructions not to open it until she returned home from the Purple Palace. MaPOP decided to follow the instructions. It was fun having one last present to open when she returned home.

As MaPOP reflected on these moments, she realized each step of her pilgrimage had been preparing her for the wonder and mystery of the Purple Palace. Every town, every friend, and even every challenge had shaped her journey. The memory of Agent Stanley's unopened gift stirred a spark of anticipation, perhaps her adventure was not truly finished yet.

Then there was Pareal. He was strange and clearly tried to visit harm and redirection on MaPOP. It was unbelievable since they had never met before. It was strange the way he appeared out of nowhere and vanished the same way. MaPOP thought to herself he had the strangest toes and shoes she had ever seen.

MaPOP spotted him (Pareal) at the town of Ping2thePong. Even though he had the opportunity to explain what would happen at 2:00, he did not. As a result of only sharing partial information, MaPOP found herself literally in the middle of a high-speed game of ping pong. It was a good thing Agent Stanley was there to help her navigate the playing field and only be sandwiched once between a Ping and a Pong. The giant brown balls were so proud of themselves for smashing into her.

The last town she visited before arriving at the Purple Palace was deep underground. It was the town of the Potato Pit. It was a dark, earthy place located underneath a huge ancient potato field. The light underground was memorable because it was an unusual purplish glow. It was everywhere MaPOP went. The magical light guided her to antique doors. MaPOP was not sure how old they were, but they seemed ancient. She chuckled to herself as she recalled the synchronized movements of the tiniest spuds called Tater Tots.

MaPOP took a deep breath. She had revisited her day's activities while seated in a luxurious grand ballroom waiting to be escorted into the purple wing of the palace where she would be introduced and have dinner with the Prince and Princess. The waiting area had stripes on the walls from ceiling to floor. The stripes alternated between gold, silver, violet, and lavender. At her side, standing tall, was Pewter. He had taken care of everything. MaPOP knew she had never looked this beautiful in her whole puppet life. Her braids which she usually sectioned into two ponytails, was curled in a sophisticated updo. The clothing she arrived in had been packed in a travel bag along with all the gifts she had taken on her adventure. She still had the package Agent Stanley had given her. Agent Stanley told her not to open it until she returned home. She thought that was strange, but everything about the whole day had been strange. Pewter advised her not to give her things a second thought. He informed her he personally would make sure she did not forget them when it was time to return home.

In that quiet moment before being announced, MaPOP realized how much her journey had changed her. Each trial, each friend, and even each danger had led her to this exact place in time. She smiled softly, ready to step into the purple wing and embrace the destiny that awaited her.

MaPOP thought of home. She was not ready to leave yet, but she did look forward to getting to know her new puppies. She recalled they were fascinating creatures, unlike any puppies she had met before. She recalled they appeared exceptionally intelligent. They played together, but they did not fight.

Her thoughts were interrupted by the activity around her. A harpsichord played a lovely melody as the double doors were opened wide by the staff. The aroma of fresh baked goods and roasted vegetables filled the air. As she entered the room, she glanced down at her fabulous silk slippers. She held the folds of her dress to avoid stepping on the exquisite fabric. She had never seen anything like it.

As she took five more steps, she almost fainted. It was the Prince and Princess. They were seated side-by-side at the head of the table. Their hairstyles made them appear very tall. Both had hairstyles piled very high in ornate "P" shaped designs. The Prince wore an assortment of twists. The Princess wore beaded and jeweled curls. They both wore lavender crushed velvet capes with large fire opal clasps. Their hair was piled high right through the center of their crowns. The Prince gently lifted his right hand, signaling Pewter to bring MaPOP closer. This was the very moment MaPOP had dreamt of since she had read the invitation. The light seemed to dim as she approached the pair of royals. It was at this time MaPOP realized she was the only guest. There were no other attendees at this dinner except the Prince, Princess, and MaPOP.

Her heart pounded with both excitement and disbelief. The grandeur of the moment pressed heavily upon her, yet she felt strangely calm, as though this meeting had been destined all along.

As MaPOP stepped forward, Pewter stepped backwards. MaPOP stopped about five paces away from the pair. Both the Prince and Princess stared at MaPOP with just the hint of a smile. MaPOP had been advised to bow and wait until she was spoken to. When she raised her puppet head, her eyes met those of the Prince.

In that instant, she sensed a kindness in his gaze that eased her worries, while the Princess's jeweled curls sparkled like a thousand stars, surrounding MaPOP with warmth and welcome.

The Prince spoke first, "Welcome MaPOP. We see you have found your way safely to the Purple Palace and arrived on time." MaPOP was star-struck. She managed to nod her head in agreement.

It was then that the Princess spoke. She asked with an inquisitive tone, "Did you have any trouble as you traveled here?"

MaPOP spoke gently. She said, "Before I respond to your inquiry, please allow me to say thank you for the wonderful gifts in the special delivery package. Thank you, I will treasure them always."

At this point, as though sharing a private thought, the Prince and Princess smiled at each other. When they returned their attention back to MaPOP, she continued. "My journey was pleasant, with the exception of a strange creature who identified himself as Pareal."

Hearing MaPOP say these words, both the Prince and the Princess laughed. Their laughter was not mocking, but knowing, carrying the weight of experience.

The Princess explained, "The creature you met is an enemy. His real name is Peril, and he is related to Pewter, whom we hold in very high regard."

It was then MaPOP remembered the wording in the special instructions stating never trust Peril. Her eyes widened as she realized she had been tricked by him. He had lied about his identity. MaPOP remained silent, nodding her head up and down.

The Prince added warmly, "But it appears Peril was no match for you. The proof is your timely arrival to our Palace."

Just then, a member of the royal staff entered the room and whispered something to Pewter. After the messenger walked away, Pewter spoke to the Prince and Princess in front of MaPOP. He announced that the final dinner guest had arrived. He inquired of the Prince and Princess whether or not the guest should join them at this time.

The Prince nodded yes. In royal fashion, Pewter took one step back, then pivoted with military precision. The simple gesture reminded MaPOP of his quiet strength and absolute loyalty.

MaPOP was impressed with the way Pewter carried himself. Returning her attention to the Prince and Princess, she stared at them with anticipation.

Then the Princess said, "Let's join our guest at the dining table."

As they both stood up from their thrones, MaPOP was surprised by their height. They seemed like trees towering over her. They were both slender. Their limbs were long. Their strides were royal, and their heads were held very high.

As they glided towards a set of double doors with an attendant on either side, MaPOP counted to herself, noting it took six of her puppet steps for every one of theirs.

As they arrived at the double doors, the attendants nodded in unison to acknowledge the superior position of the Prince and Princess. Simultaneously, they opened the doors in a perfectly synchronized manner.

For MaPOP, the moment felt like stepping into a dream, one she had carried in her puppet heart since the day she first read the royal invitation.

MaPOP gasped as she took in the panoramic view through the open windows. Following the Prince and Princess, she looked around the room and observed large portraits of several woodland animals. Each painting seemed almost alive, their eyes following her every movement as though silently welcoming her.

The Prince and Princess headed towards a balcony. Looking past their towering silhouettes, MaPOP saw a beautifully decorated table with several glowing candelabras. A few more paces onto the balcony, she counted four place settings on the table.

The Prince was seated first, with the aid of an attendant, at the head of the table. The Princess was seated at the other end of the table by another attendant. Once seated, they made eye contact with each other and smiled. MaPOP could feel the love they shared for one another. It seemed to hang in the air, fragrant and intoxicating.

MaPOP was then seated, and the final dinner guest was ushered into the room. To her astonishment, it was Agent Stanley, but she was not wearing the purple beanie. Agent Stanley had undergone a complete makeover. Her purple beanie was replaced with lots of pin curls. Her ears had been fluffed, and her face was carefully made up. Her nails had been painted to match the magenta gown she wore.

The gown was embroidered with pheasants, peacocks, and exotic birds. MaPOP thought to herself that Agent Stanley looked like she belonged here at the palace. She wore a confidence that was quite appropriate for this engagement. There was no trace of the mysterious bunny from the woods, only elegance, grace, and poise.

She glided across the room with familiarity, clearly showing she had been here before. After the four were seated, the Prince motioned for another attendant to announce the evening's menu.

It was a very classy affair, and MaPOP enjoyed every moment of it. The golden glow of the candelabras flickered softly across their faces, making the scene feel timeless, like a memory that would never fade.

The attendant announced the evening's menu from memory. First, they were served a butternut squash soup, served warm and topped with chives, sour cream, and just a touch of smoked paprika.

The next course was served on individual plates. It was a bed of assorted greens, arugula and romaine, laced with shredded carrots, white straw mushrooms, and garlic-stuffed olives. Clearly, MaPOP was the only one at the table not accustomed to such delicacies. She smiled politely, determined to keep pace with the elegant company, even though each flavor was so new to her puppet palate. Little did she know they were just getting started.

MaPOP was already beginning to feel full, even though they were each served small portions. She was committed to powering through the opulent meal all the way to the end. The next course of the menu was a bit spicy. It was lentil croquettes with a yogurt sauce. Each person at the table stated they were absolutely delicious.

Next, the attendants presented an eggplant and black olive stew. The broth of the stew was rich and flavored with ginger, cumin, and golden raisins. The attendant squeezed a fresh lemon wedge into each bowl.

The almost last course was a chickpea pot pie, which included bell peppers, celery, mushrooms, onions, cream cheese, fresh sage, chickpeas, and a flaky butter crust. The presentation was delightful. The pot pie was shaped into a letter "P." MaPOP chuckled quietly to herself at the thought that even dinner was dressed in purple palace perfection. They all ate and ate and ate, and MaPOP began to be concerned she would explode from all the wonderful food she had eaten.

Just then, the Princess suggested they go inside for dessert and tea. The attendants pulled their chairs back and guided each of them by their hands back through the double doors.

This time, they sat in a much smaller area. It was quite cozy. There were four comfortable chairs positioned around a hexagon-shaped table. MaPOP knew to wait and allow the Prince and Princess to sit down first.

MaPOP glanced at Agent Stanley quickly. Agent Stanley was already looking at her and winked one of her bunny eyes, as though something else was going to happen. MaPOP's puppet heart skipped a beat; she knew Agent Stanley's wink always meant a secret surprise.

The attendants returned with caramelized pumpkin and persimmon scones drizzled with decadent white chocolate. The scones were large, and the staff sliced them and presented each guest with a slice on a golden plate.

The cinnamon tea was the perfect complement for the pumpkin and persimmon scones. MaPOP took one bite and gently placed the dessert plate back on the table. She smiled a satisfied smile at the Prince first and then nodded her great pleasure to the Princess.

The warmth of the tea, the sweetness of the scone, and the glow of the cozy room made MaPOP feel as if she were wrapped in a dream. But the wink from Agent Stanley lingered in her thoughts, hinting that the evening's story was not quite finished.

Even though they made light conversation during the meal, MaPOP intuitively understood an important conversation would follow. After taking several bites of the fresh-baked scones, the Prince placed his dessert plate down and began to study MaPOP's facial expression. MaPOP nodded; she was ready to hear whatever the Prince needed to say.

He began by saying, "MaPOP, the Princess and I have a need for another Agent to support the work Agent Stanley has begun. Your interview took place today, and we are quite pleased with the way you conducted yourself. You showed cunning and kindness, both are very important for the opportunity we are presenting to you today."

MaPOP leaned forward to make sure she was hearing the information correctly. The Prince continued, "In one of our provinces, just outside of the area you are now familiar with, a brewing problem has begun. Agent Stanley has submitted her preliminary report after her own exploration. It appears two factions have developed a strong dislike for each other. One of these communities is significantly stronger than the other. We will not tolerate a war in our provinces for any reason."

He paused briefly, his tone serious, then went on. "The Princess and I agree: if two Special Agents are dispatched immediately, we can understand the root cause of the problem, mediate, and avoid further casualties."

Then the Princess leaned forward and asked MaPOP directly, "Are you interested in this opportunity to become a member of the royal court, serving as a Special Agent? If you accept our offer, you will be the second Special Agent in the history of our royal reign. MaPOP, what are your thoughts on this opportunity we are presenting to you?"

MaPOP's puppet heart skipped a beat. She had expected a royal adventure, but not a lifelong responsibility. The weight of the Princess's words pressed on her, yet at the same time, an undeniable spark of excitement flared inside her. This was more than an invitation, it was a calling.

MaPOP was shocked. She did not see this coming at all. This new information presented a context for the very valuable gifts and the unexpected appearances of Agent Stanley earlier in the day. MaPOP knew this was a very important decision. She was tempted to answer yes right away, but instead, she asked the Prince and Princess for a few days to think about their offer.

MaPOP then asked an important question. "What exactly is a Special Agent?"

The Prince and Princess smiled at each other when they heard her question. They both looked at Agent Stanley. Agent Stanley stared directly at the Prince and Princess and nodded her head one time without speaking.

The Prince continued, "That is an excellent question. I think it is fitting for Agent Stanley to spend a few days with you. Agent Stanley can answer your question as well as give you more background information on the Province we have mentioned. She has traveled throughout our kingdom, is well respected, and is a master at disguising herself."

MaPOP's curiosity deepened. She could feel the weight of the responsibility being offered to her, but she also felt reassured knowing Agent Stanley, someone she had already begun to trust, would guide her through the unknown.

The Prince motioned for an attendant to approach him. Pewter walked forward and stood by the Prince's side. The Prince gave Pewter instructions to make sure MaPOP arrived home safely.

After saying this, both the Prince and Princess stood up. They smiled warmly at MaPOP and asked Agent Stanley to see them before she departed. Agent Stanley nodded her compliance, and the Prince and Princess excused themselves. The Prince was holding the Princess's hand as they exited through the doors opened by other attendants.

As MaPOP watched them leave, she felt both honored and overwhelmed. The grandeur of the Purple Palace was behind her now, but her journey was far from over. What lay ahead was a path she could never have imagined.

MaPOP looked at Agent Stanley. Agent Stanley said, "You can expect a visit from me in two days." Then Pewter asked MaPOP to follow him. He had the bag with all her belongings in his hand.

MaPOP, still in shock, stood up and followed Pewter. Agent Stanley remained seated at the table. Pewter directed MaPOP to follow him down a narrow corridor. The further they walked, the darker it seemed to get. At the end of the corridor was a doorway with a large cabinet next to it. Pewter handed MaPOP her bag and told her to wait where she was standing. MaPOP wondered if she was dreaming, it had all been so wonderful.

Pewter returned with a flute similar to the flute MaPOP had received the previous day. Next, Pewter pulled small shiny objects from his pocket. He placed both objects in his mouth and began to play a melody. The door in front of them opened. While still playing the flute, Pewter moved his head in the direction of the open door. MaPOP understood he wanted her to cross the threshold. Pewter followed close behind her.

He was still playing the melody when the wall on the other side of the threshold disappeared. MaPOP gasped, they were back in a portal. When he stopped playing, she was standing in front of her building. Pewter waved goodbye and began playing the flute again. He vanished in a split second.

It was dark outside. MaPOP's head was spinning from the day's activities. She looked around and determined everything was exactly the way she had left it. She took a few steps, opened the door, and wondered if it was too late to disturb her neighbor and retrieve her puppies.

It had been a special day. MaPOP would take her time to savor each moment while she prepared for Agent Stanley's visit. MaPOP thought to herself, *"Am I ready to be a Special Agent for the Prince and Princess of the Purple Palace?"*

Her heart fluttered as she considered the question. Tomorrow would be an ordinary day once again, or so it would seem. But deep down, MaPOP knew life could never truly be ordinary after such an extraordinary adventure. Somewhere in the shadows of the Purple Kingdom, more mysteries awaited, and her story was only just beginning.

The End.